HOW TO

EXPAND

YOUR
YOUTH
MINISTRY

YOUTH SPECIALTIES TITLES

Professional Resources
Compassionate Kids
Developing Spiritual Growth in Junior High Students
Equipped to Serve
Help! I'm a Volunteer Youth Worker!
Help! I'm a Sunday School Teacher!
How to Expand Your Youth Ministry
How to Recruit and Train Volunteer Youth Workers
Junior High Ministry (Revised Edition)
The Ministry of Nurture
One Kid at a Time
Peer Counseling in Youth Groups
Advanced Peer Counseling in Youth Groups

Discussion Starter Resources
Get 'Em Talking
High School TalkSheets
Junior High TalkSheets
High School TalkSheets: Psalms and Proverbs
Junior High TalkSheets: Psalms and Proverbs
More High School TalkSheets
More Junior High TalkSheets
Parent Ministry TalkSheets
What If . . . ?
Would You Rather . . . ?

Ideas Library
Ideas Combo 1-4, 5-8, 9-12, 13-16, 17-20, 21-24, 25-28, 29-32, 33-36, 37-40, 41-44, 45-48, 49-
    52, 53, 54, 55
Ideas Index

Youth Ministry Programming
Compassionate Kids
Creative Bible Lessons in John: Encounters with Jesus
Creative Bible Lessons on the Life of Christ
Creative Programming Ideas for Junior High Ministry
Creative Socials and Special Events
Dramatic Pauses
Facing Your Future
Great Fundraising Ideas for Youth Groups
Great Ideas for Small Youth Groups
Great Retreats for Youth Groups
Greatest Skits on Earth
Greatest Skits on Earth, Volume 2
Hot Illustrations for Youth Talks
Hot Talks

Junior High Game Nights
More Junior High Game Nights
More Hot Illustrations for Youth Talks
Play It! Great Games for Groups
Play It Again! More Great Games for Groups
Road Trip
Super Sketches for Youth Ministry
Teaching the Bible Creatively
Up Close and Personal: How to Build Community in Your Youth Group

Clip Art
ArtSource Volume 1—Fantastic Activities
ArtSource Volume 2—Borders, Symbols, Holidays, and Attention Getters
ArtSource Volume 3—Sports
ArtSource Volume 4—Phrases and Verses
ArtSource Volume 5—Amazing Oddities and Appalling Images
ArtSource Volume 6—Spiritual Topics
ArtSource Volume 7—Variety Pack

Video
Edge TV
The Heart of Youth Ministry: A Morning with Mike Yaconelli
Next Time I Fall in Love Video Curriculum
Promo Spots for Junior High Game Nights
Resource Seminar Video Series
Understanding Your Teenager Video Curriculum

Student Books
Grow for It Journal
Grow for It Journal through the Scriptures
Next Time I Fall in Love
101 Things to Do During a Dull Sermon
Wild Truth Journal for Junior Highers

90984

HOW TO

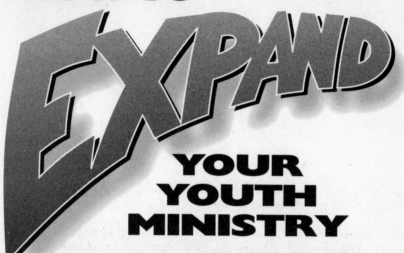

EXPAND

YOUR
YOUTH
MINISTRY

PRACTICAL WAYS TO
INCREASE YOUR
ATTENDANCE

LEN KAGELER

Youth
Specialties

ZondervanPublishingHouse
Grand Rapids, Michigan

A Division of HarperCollinsPublishers

How to Expand Your Youth Ministry: Practical ways to increase your attendance
Copyright © 1996 by Youth Specialties, Inc.

Youth Specialties Books, 1224 Greenfield Drive, El Cajon, California 92021, are
published by Zondervan Publishing House, 5300 Patterson, S.E., Grand Rapids,
Michigan 49530.

Library of Congress Cataloging-in-Publication Data

Kageler, Len, 1950-
    How to expand your youth ministry : practical ways to increase your attendance /
Len Kageler
        p.   cm.
    Included bibliographical references.
    ISBN 0-310-20778-9 (pbk.)
    1. Church group work with youth.   I. Title.
BV4447.K352 1996
259'.23—dc20   95-39803
                                                                            CIP

Edited by Noel Becchetti and Vicki Newby
Typography and Design by PAZ Design Group

Printed in the United States of America

96 97 98 99/ /4 3 2 1

To my wife Janet...

who models Christlikeness to me

day in, day out.

TABLE OF CONTENTS

C H A P T E R

1

CHAPTER

YOUTH GROUP ATTENDANCE

the big picture

The longer he talked, the worse I felt.

"We've got about five hundred coming to youth group. The group continues to grow rapidly. New people want to come back because they like the programs and love all the excitement. Many come to Christ each week. And the best part is, the whole program is planned and led by the kids themselves. They do everything. They're totally in charge."

He went on about his wonderful group for nearly an hour.

Did I sit there saying to myself, "Praise God, the Lord is really blessing his ministry. It's so great that such good things are happening. I'm so happy for this youth pastor!"? Not exactly.

I was skeptical, jealous, envious, and most of all, depressed. Not only was I depressed, I felt very guilty. The conclusion I reached was: "I am one crummy youth pastor. Here I am, struggling to get a handful of kids out on Wednesday night, and this guy has 40 kids just doing the media for his programs. Why don't I wake up to reality and quit? I'll never really make it."

I've met a lot of youth workers who feel inferior because their numbers don't compare well with other youth groups. In fact, most youth workers feel this way. We look at our own group with a picture in the back of our minds of a huge youth group somewhere else where everything is "successful."

Then one morning, it hit me. "That guy said they had ten thousand people in their Sunday services. That means he's only got five percent of that number coming out to youth group. With a church of ten thousand he'd better have that many in youth group or something is wrong! We've got ten percent of our Sunday morning number coming out. Hey, I'm not so bad after all!"

My guilt and remorse melted away. This insight, and many others that have followed through the years, have made a huge difference in how I look at youth groups and youth ministry.

BY THE NUMBERS

This book takes a practical look at increasing youth ministry attendance. We may say we're not concerned about numbers. We may say we're not caught up in an unspiritual success syndrome. We may pretend to ignore the numbers. But let's face it—the numbers matter. All of us surely prefer numerical growth to decline. Growth affirms that we're doing something right. It's a sign that God is blessing. Those of us who receive paychecks from our churches are smart enough to know that if the right numbers aren't there, we're out of jobs.

In this book, we'll look at a number of factors that impact how many kids show up at our meetings, events, and activities. We'll see that some are, quite frankly, beyond our control, while we can directly influence others.

We won't stop with just analysis—we'll also consider practical and workable ways to overcome specific barriers to youth group attendance growth. This won't be an encyclopedia of gimmicks like cash rebates for youth group attendance! These attendance-building ideas have integrity and have worked in real live youth groups around the country.

Research for this book carried me in a lot of directions, but my main source of information is a survey prepared especially for the 1994 National Youth Workers Conventions in Chicago and San Diego.

In studying youth ministry attendance, I've had many "aha" experiences. Things I've observed during twenty-five years of youth ministry have become understandable in the light of hard data. Speaking of hard data, following are some facts and figures that may bring a smile or a frown.

CHURCH ATTENDANCE EQUALS YOUTH MINISTRY ATTENDANCE

How many people attend your church? It is a simple and complicated question at the same time. In the 1994 survey, "church attendance" meant combined Sunday morning and/or Saturday night turnout. "Youth group attendance" meant the number of students that show up at a non-Sunday school function that is considered the main gathering of the group.

Take a moment to ponder the charts on page 14. Now you can see why I eventually felt so good after talking with my mega-church friend. If church attendance is in the 450 to 750 range, attendance for each age bracket will likely be between thirty and forty students. If a thousand or more people attend church, the youth ministry will likely be in the 100-plus category.

It is interesting, isn't it, that youth group attendance seems to plateau at thirty to forty. Why? More on that in Chapter Four.

UPS AND DOWNS

When I first got into youth ministry in Seattle, Washington, I envisioned that growth in my youth group would start slow, then, gathering speed like a rocket, soar higher and higher. My attendance graph would show dramatic, even exponential growth.

In reality, my stats didn't exactly rocket skyward. I blamed it on my

WORSHIP ATTENDANCE & YOUTH MINISTRY NUMBERS (Junior High School)		
Church Size	Average Sun. School Attendance	Main Youth Group Meeting
99-150	9	11
151-250	13	13
251-350	20	20
351-450	24	26
451-550	24	30
551-750	38	38
751-1000	41	41
1000-1250	55	51

WORSHIP ATTENDANCE & YOUTH MINISTRY NUMBERS (Senior High School)		
Church Size	Average Sun. School Attendance	Main Youth Group Meeting
99-150	10	9
151-250	14	15
251-350	16	20
351-450	26	27
451-550	25	30
551-750	36	40
751-1000	41	38
1000-1250	60	51

predecessor. I had inherited some dysfunctional kids and it wasn't my fault that the group didn't grow as long as they were still around.

By the end of the fourth year, however, the problem kids had graduated. Now I had no one to blame but me! By then, I had noticed a distinct attendance pattern. Group attendance was good in the fall, a little better in the winter, down in the spring, and way down in the summer. I figured it had to do with Seattle weather. Once the sun started to shine, kids found outdoor activities more attractive than youth group.

Then I began to compare the current fall with previous years, and so on through the seasons. That gave me a truer picture of year-to-year growth or decline. Growth was modest, but at least it was growth.

A few months later, our senior pastor resigned. I subsequently saw my numbers drop from the previous year, as did attendance at Sunday morning worship. This gave me another "aha" experience: Growth and decline in youth ministry attendance is closely linked to the ups and downs of Sunday morning attendance.

My "up and down" experience in Seattle, according to research, is a nationwide reality. Among the 460 churches represented in the survey, if worship attendance was up, so was youth group attendance. The opposite was also true. A decline in worship attendance generally meant youth group numbers would similarly sink.

As a church grows, the pool of people who have teenagers increases. Some, though not all, of these will want to attend youth group. Our attendance and total pool of church kids both increase accordingly.

BOOM TIME

Speaking of a growing pool, the children of the Baby Boomers (those born between 1944 and 1964) began entering early adolescence en masse in the early 1990s. This demographic tidal wave has risen through the elementary schools and has washed up to the shores of junior and senior high schools. This teenage high tide will continue for another fifteen years before it recedes. Churches with effective youth ministries can expect to flourish during this demographic surge.

ATTENDANCE AND GOD'S PRIORITIES

On many levels, youth group attendance is a spiritual issue. It certainly affects our spirits. Who can deny that we feel better when numbers are high than when numbers are low? If youth group went well and my attendance was high, I felt thankful to God, happy to be in ministry, useful, and at peace. I looked forward to my day off as a chance to be refreshed and get ready for more. If things did not go well (numerically or otherwise), I became sullen, running endless "what ifs" through my mind. My day off became an escape to get away and gain perspective.

Our attitudes about numbers is a spiritual issue. I have had the privilege of knowing several professional and volunteer youth ministers who have engaged in youth work for more than two decades. They all speak of seasons in youth group life. There are times when everything seems to come together. Dynamic volunteer leadership is in place, the "in" kids in the group are both spiritual and outgoing, and the ministry seems like a vital, healthy organism.

The youth group is reminiscent of the early church where "every day they continued to meet together . . . with glad and sincere hearts, praising God and enjoying the favor of all the people. And the Lord added to their number daily those who were being saved" (Acts 2:46-47). Mature youth workers, however, have learned not to place too much emotional stock in such success.

There are other seasons when the youth group resembles the early church in different ways—racked by conflict, discontent, apathy—all throwing a thick lead blanket over the radiation of the Spirit (see Acts 15). These tough times force us to take a look both inward and upward. Spiritually, we remind ourselves that God calls us to faithfulness, service, and graciousness that models how God loves us. We try to remember that God cares about us regardless of how many kids come to our meetings. There is a way of experiencing God that only seems to come when our hearts are broken. For better or worse, we get ample opportunity to experience this phenomenon in youth ministry.

BAPTISM BLUES

I remember the time I told the pastoral staff of my church that at least twelve high schoolers, and probably fifteen to twenty, would be involved in the next baptism service. I'd been in the position for eighteen months and had learned that no youth had been baptized in the two years previous to my coming. At least, I thought, our leadership core would jump at the chance.

With great enthusiasm, I outlined the opportunity to my kids and gave them the opportunity to respond. Four said yes, one said maybe, two were vehemently opposed, and the rest just seemed apathetic.

When baptism Sunday finally came around, I had recovered enough to enjoy the service and to be thankful for those who were baptized instead of angry at those who weren't. My attitude had to go through a spiritual pilgrimage from disappointment and anger to understanding and gratitude.

Then there was the time a good friend of mine called in despair. He had scheduled a mega junior high retreat, with projected attendance in the eighty to one hundred range. The date was locked in, the deposit sent. Then the large Christian school his church runs changed the date of its spring junior high basketball tournament to the same weekend as his retreat without bothering to check the church calendar. The publicity had been mailed, plans made, teams signed up. The tournament, too, was in cement. There went all the jocks (real and aspiring) as well as the cheerleaders (real and wannabees) of his youth group. His retreat attendance ended up at twenty-five. His financial break-even point was fifty.

Most of us have faced attendance-related disappointments, some stemming from circumstances like I've just described. For many of us, however, we must come to terms with youth ministries that have plateaued or are in decline.

HOPE AND HELP

This is a book of both hope and help. We gain hope as we understand the factors that impact the health of our youth ministries. We gain help as we deal practically, issue by issue, with what can be done in real-world situations. Many of those who took the survey also wrote insightful comments which I will pass along.

Before talking about expanding our youth ministries, however, let's first understand why some are resistant to the very idea of growth.

WHY GROUPS ARE GROWING

■ "Our kids are moving up through the church, those kids are inviting friends, and we have families coming to the church looking for a youth group for their kids." *(New York)*

■ "The growth of the overall junior high population in my area." *(Missouri)*

■ "One of our church's key objectives is to reach out to families and God is blessing!" *(Maryland)*

■ "We have worked very hard to build personal relationships with the kids in the group." *(Tennessee)*

WHY GROUPS ARE NOT GROWING

■ "Our church split and is now three separate congregations." *(Michigan)*

■ "The church is in a maintenance mode—there is not a vision for outreach and growth. This automatically leads to decline throughout." *(Iowa)*

■ "Three years ago our senior high averaged twenty-five at meetings. Now we average fifteen. Most of our senior highers have graduated and the younger kids haven't caught up yet." *(Washington)*

FOR WHAT IT'S WORTH

■ "Our youth ministry has gone from a handful to an average attendance of over seventy. Our senior pastor is very supportive of the youth group but I think the real key is this: I phone every kid every week. It takes five to six hours each week now. Other volunteers are getting involved in this weekly phoning so we can keep growing." *(Florida)*

CHAPTER 2

OVERCOMING
growth anxiety

It was one of those multichurch youth events that turned out well. Hundreds of kids arrived from thirty different churches and, amazingly, there was some mixing going on. Kids of different churches were talking with each other. When it came time to load the bowling-alley-bound vans, mine filled up mostly with kids I'd never seen before.

Tami climbed into the shotgun seat next to me. She was quite a talker! As we drove to the bowling alley, she spoke warmly of her youth group. They did so many things together.

"Say, Ranger Len," Tami queried, "how many are in your youth group?"

"Oh, I'd say about one hundred fifty if they were all in one place at the same time," I replied as I maneuvered through traffic. Her eyes got as big as quarters.

"Wow! How many are here today?"

"Oh, I think we've got twelve."

Tami nearly flipped out of her seat. She couldn't believe it and expressed her amazement in various ways. I finally asked, "Say Tami, how many are in your group?"

"Ten," she said, "and we don't go anywhere unless we can all go."

Tami's joy in her youth group was principally because it was small. She wouldn't want to see her group double, triple, or grow to a list of one hundred fifty names on some roster in the church office.

If you are convinced that the Bible mandates a concern for reaching out, and that successful outreach results in numerical growth, it is important to understand why others are not excited about that same prospect.

GROWTH = CHANGE = LOSS

You and I may not agree that change equals loss, but some of our people will. What do people have to lose if the youth group grows?

The kids lose a close-knit, comfortable youth group where everyone feels good about everyone else. Their school can be a confusing and stress-producing place, but in youth group they know what and whom to expect. The big-fish-in-a-small-pond leaders may lose their official or unofficial leadership roles in the group.

The adult volunteers lose the comfort of knowing everyone, being known, and knowing what to expect. As volunteers, we often come to youth group tired, our minds full of the problems and concerns of the day we just survived. Our work lives provide us with all the change, stress, and challenge we can handle. We help at youth group because we love kids and know we should be involved in ministry. A growing youth ministry may threaten our own comfort level.

Parents of churched kids aren't always wild about the idea of a growing youth ministry. A major reason parents choose a church is to have the needs of their kids met. A growing youth group may dilute the level of personal care received by their churched children.

The church board may see a growing youth ministry as additional wear and tear on the building, pressure to increase the youth budget, and requests for big-ticket capital expenses like vans. It may mean complaints about cigarette butts in the parking lot and missing items from the food pantry. Also, board members don't enjoy hearing about the dissatisfaction of parents who feel their kids aren't being ministered to.

In my book *The Youth Minister's Survival Guide*[1] I presented the cases of 185 youth pastors who had been fired by their churches. Of these, forty-two percent were in youth groups that had grown numerically in the previous twelve months. And some of these were fired specifically because of that growth. One pastor reported:

"We fired Bob because he had no heart for the kids from church families. He was excellent at attracting and winning non-church kids, and our group grew from twenty to eighty in the three years he was here. But the group got so lopsided that our church kids didn't feel comfortable in their own group. We have several parents of teens on the church board and I had to agree with them. We needed to go in a different direction."

This doesn't have to happen! It is possible to have a growing youth group without alienating kids, parents, volunteers, or the church board.

REMEDY #1: UNDERSTAND THE IMPACT OF CHANGE

If we understand the dynamics of change, we are better able to speak to the hearts of those who are fearful of growth.

Dr. Robert Anderson of Western Baptist Seminary reminds us why people resist change[2]:

- Change is uncomfortable for them.
- They are not convinced that change is necessary.
- They lack confidence in their leaders.
- They do not own the proposed change.
- They are uncertain where the proposed change will lead.
- They are tired of continuous change.
- They are afraid of losing something.

It isn't hard to envision these reasons applying to some youths, parents, staff, or board members.

However, Dr. Anderson also points out that people will change, and even change happily, when other things are true:[3]

- They are convinced change is legitimate.
- They see the old system as no longer meeting their needs.
- They know that they no longer have the answers.
- Their attitudes have been changed.

So we should not boldly announce that it's our goal to see the youth group double in the next four weeks. Instead, we should proceed carefully, understanding the fears that some have and utilizing the three additional remedies that follow.

REMEDY #2: REACH THE REACHED BEFORE REACHING THE LOST

It's true. Most church people have the nerve to believe that our job, whether we are volunteers or get paid, is to first reach the church kids. This must be our solid foundation before we place major emphasis on outreach and numerical growth. If we have no heart for our churched kids, we had better find a different ministry. Young Life, Youth For Christ, Fellowship of Christian Athletes, and other parachurch organizations provide ample opportunities for volunteers and full-timers to channel their passion for lost kids.

I am not saying we need to automatically bail out of church-based youth ministry if we have a heart for the lost. I am saying integrity demands that we bail if we have no heart for the found. I have met church-based youth workers who seem to loathe church kids. Yes, these kids can be apathetic, unmotivated complainers; but they also can be transformed by God into motivated world-changers.

"Reaching the reached first" is a vital component of the Sonlife Strategy. Sonlife holds seminars around the country on what it takes to build a Great Commission mindset and ministry.[4] They point out that Christ's ministry had a foundational/preparatory phase before he majored on outreach. Principles of this foundational phase applied to youth ministry include:

- Creating an atmosphere of love—through leaders showing they care in tangible ways, and creating bonding experiences for those in the group.
- Building a healthy group image—through successful programming that

kids own and feel proud of.
- Establishing a contacting ministry—by leaders taking the time to meet kids on their own turf.
- Communicating a proper concept of Christ—in teaching and modeling Christlikeness.
- Building a prayer base—both in the group and for the group.
- Communicating the Word and helping students understand how to feed themselves.

Sonlife cautions that moving prematurely into outreach without fully establishing the foundation means potential for frustration and failure.

REMEDY #3: CREATE STRUCTURE THAT IS GEARED FOR CARE

Anxiety on the part of students, parents, and staff is greatly reduced if it is obvious that your ministry is structured to promote care and shepherding. The following short quiz will test your insight into this important remedy:

Question: One of the best ways to structure a youth ministry for care and meeting of needs is . . .

___A. through small groups

___B. through small groups

___C. through small groups

___D. all of the above

Very good! I have seen volunteers and paid youth workers burn out or get fired because they couldn't figure this out.

Jim was the ultimate up-front personality, an excellent speaker, dynamic, and a kids-flock-to-him youth worker. And flock those kids did! Unfortunately for Jim and his volunteer staff, he was unable to gear his group for care. Kids were attracted to Jim and his charisma, but he was too busy to help them with their personal problems. His staff was like a revolving door; they were recruited to help with the youth ministry but all they did was come and watch Jim do his thing. It is very intimidating for most adults to come to a group with one hundred-plus kids and just "hang out" or "try to build relationships!" Eventually, it all fell apart. Jim couldn't handle the nuts-and-bolts administration of a large group, kids got disillusioned, and staff quit in frustration. I have seen many groups like Jim's—spectacular growth followed by collapse.

Successful structuring for care can be configured in many ways. In the junior high group where I am a volunteer, we spend ten minutes each Wednesday night in small groups. Each leader has the same group each week. All the kids know who their leaders are. All the parents know who the leaders are for their sons and daughters. The leaders try to phone the kids throughout the week to see how they are doing and to let them know they are missed when they are absent.

I was the youth pastor of a church in Seattle for fourteen years. We considered our group to be the 150 senior highers who would show up to some event in a typical month. Even with a group that most would consider large, we rarely had complaints about kids not being cared for. It was obvious to both kids and parents that each student was part of a twenty to thirty member team that was shepherded by three adult volunteers. Kids felt cared for. We weren't asking leaders to care about everyone, just those on their team. Staff felt useful. They didn't come to watch me do my thing; they came to connect with and care for their youth group within the youth group. Parents felt their kids were cared for since adult leaders on their team called and teams did special things on their own throughout the year. (Our team structure is more fully described in Chapter Six.)

With the team structure, there is no theoretical limit to how large a group can grow. Teams or small groups can meet on Sunday mornings, in the context of a midweek meeting, or off the church property during the week. The concept can be sliced, diced, and served up in a variety of ways, but some kind of small group structure assures kids, staff, and parents that personal care is happening.

REMEDY #4: TEACHING/TRAINING WITH A VISION FOR OUTREACH, COUPLED WITH DOABLE OUTREACH OPPORTUNITIES

It does not require a seminary degree to see that the Bible is full of God's heart for outreach. As we unpack this among our staff and students, the question becomes obvious: "So what are we going to do about it?"

Once a teenager starts to grow in her or his Christian life and begins to understand that the benefits of this life go way beyond fire insurance, their desire to have friends experience the Good News follows naturally.

In Chapter Five I describe the workings of a youth cabinet. Most of the members express a desire to see their friends start coming to youth group and find Christ. They are often reminded of God's heart for outreach through the normal teaching that takes place.

We keep the idea of outreach before them in additional ways:

■ Each cabinet member has a Five Most Wanted list of non-Christian friends. As a cabinet, we pray for these people regularly. (A side benefit of this cabinet prayer is that when these guests show up at a youth event, we know who they are!)

■ When we have a special outreach event each cabinet member commits to invite one or two of their Five Most Wanted. We are accountable to one another and provide updates as the big event nears.

■ The cabinet does all the planning for events, so when we designate an occasion specifically for outreach, we ask the hard questions: "Will I invite my friend to this? Is this something my friends will enjoy?"

When these friends come, and when some do decide to follow Christ, it's time to party! The success the cabinet sees motivates them for more. Their enthusiasm spreads to others in the youth group. The above ideas, of course, do not have to be limited to a youth cabinet. They can include any in the youth ministry who are ready for the challenge of reaching out.

If you don't have the skill or time to put together outreach training material, don't despair. Several alternatives are available.

We can take our kids to outreach training events. There are nationally-marketed events that combine inspiration, fun, outreach training, and hands-on experience. These include Sonlife Evangelism and Missions Project, New York Go, and Operation Good News.[5]

I took a group of willing but scared-to-death high schoolers to an Operation Good News event on the New Jersey shore. Each morning began with training in apologetics (answering questions non-Christians have about the Gospel) and then training in how to share the Gospel. After lunch, we hit the beaches and boardwalks along a seventy-mile stretch of the New Jersey coast, including Atlantic City. We regrouped in the late afternoon to report our experiences. Evening was for recreation, worship, and challenge. The 360 youths attending that week of camp led 425 people to Christ. Many times I heard kids say, "This has been the best week of my life!" This is a good reminder: Teenagers like to feel useful and that they are making a difference. Few things can match the contagious enthusiasm of a kid who has just had the joy of being the tool God uses to usher another person into the kingdom.

The most widely-marketed national outreach training event is Youth For Christ's triennial DC/LA event. Over 25,000 kids and adults attended the gatherings in 1994. Though hands-on witnessing experience was not offered, kids felt encouraged and motivated to take it home.[6]

We don't have to attend a camp or convention to plug into excellent motivation and training for outreach. Josh McDowell's video series *See You At the Party* got good reviews around the country as it was shown in hundreds of youth groups.[7]

What if we have no kids in the youth ministry who are ready to attend (and pay for) a DC/LA or a New York Go experience? Don't give up! Keep teaching about God's heart for outreach and consider taking your group to a major outreach event or concert that another church in your area is sponsoring. Many churches in the country are within a two-hour drive of a large church that has a youth ministry doing great things when it comes to outreach programming. Contact the youth pastor, find out what the schedule is, and get permission to come. On your first visit, don't have your group members bring friends. If the event is a positive experience, they'll want to bring friends on your second visit!

WHY GROUPS ARE GROWING

- "The power of God through direct and foundational Bible study has spurred the kids to be excited and concerned about their school friends." *(Missouri)*
- "The kids! They want to share about what's going on." *(Michigan)*
- "For junior high, focusing on our churched teens and asking them to invite newcomers to our crazy outreach evenings!" *(California)*
- "A new willingness to reach outside to unchurched neighborhood kids and to love and accept them for who they are." *(Nevada)*

WHY GROUPS ARE NOT GROWING

- "Parents leaving the church because of poor leadership in youth ministry." *(Washington)*
- "Administratively centered ministry. Youth are spectators, not owners or ministers." *(Iowa)*
- "Poor leadership, lack of organization, bad financial decisions, and an ineffective youth director. I'm the new director. I started three months ago." *(Illinois)*

FOR WHAT IT'S WORTH

"Our attendance has doubled in the last year to 60. We started doing "mundane" tasks more creatively. For announcements, I take a video camera to different places the kids know, like the mall, and video the announcements there. Sometimes I video complete strangers giving the announcements. It's fun and the kids don't know what to expect from week to week." *(Minnesota)*

END NOTES

1. Len Kageler, *Youth Minister's Survival Guide* (El Cajon, CA: Youth Specialties/Zondervan, 1991).

2. Robert Anderson, *Circle of Influence* (Chicago: Moody, 1991), 168-176.

3. Ibid., 178-180.

4. For more information contact Sonlife at (800)770-GROW.

5. For more information the organizatons may be reached at the following phone numbers: Sonlife, (800)770-GROW; New York Go, (212)567-1678; Operation Good News (Youth Department of the Christian and Missionary Alliance), (719)599-5999.

6. For more information contact Youth for Christ at (303)843-9000.

7. For more information contact Powerlink Resources at (800)336-7770.

3

YOUR PERSONALITY

(and how it impacts growth)

I'm always thankful for opportunities given to me to lead seminars for youth workers. One of my favorite topics has a title that is a mouthful: "Understanding Your God-Given Personality as a Key in Being Set Free and Unleashed to Serve with Enthusiastic Joy."

My seminar title is a mouthful, but the basic idea is short and sweet: God has given us our personalities. We know from Psalm 139 that God designed us and this grand design has to do with our whole being, not just our bodies. Understanding the strengths and weaknesses of our personality packages gives us tremendous encouragement. I've seen people light up like Christmas trees when they realized they could be glad for who they are instead of sad for who they aren't.

UNDERSTANDING YOURS

Personality differences have been a subject of curiosity and speculation for millennia. Hippocrates began the labeling process 2,500 years ago, and today, temperament theory receives much academic attention. A few decades ago it was fashionable to recognize temperament differences as simply the result of upbringing and environment. Today, however, many researchers see a strong biologic determinant in how our personalities are shaped.[1]

We're different because we were created different. Why would God want people to be different? One doesn't have to be a theologian to understand that each person is to have a different function in the body of Christ. The teaching of Scripture on spiritual gifts is clear about this (see Ephesians 4, 1 Corinthians 12, and Romans 12).

We see personality differences all around us. My three children, all teenagers now, are very different. The kids in my junior high group are amazingly different. Members of our volunteer staff are quite different. This is great! Some kids connect best with Anthony, some with Mike, some with Allison, some with me, and so on.

My favorite way of explaining personality differences is by using the labels *Lions, Otters, Golden Retrievers*, and *Beavers*.[2]

- *Lions* are leaders and can be aggressive. They like to make decisions and make things happen.
- *Otters* are life-of-the-party, fun loving, people-persons who love to make wide social contacts.

■ *Golden Retrievers* are deeply relational and sensitive. They love to get inside the head and heart of another person.
■ *Beavers* love to be factual, organized, and analytical. They make decisions comfortably only when they have all the facts in front of them.

Most youth workers I've met are strong in one or two of these areas. In the survey given at the Youth Specialties '94 Conventions, respondents reported their main personality type as follows:

Lions....................29%
Otters..................29%
Golden Retrievers 29%
Beavers.................12%

To better understand these four "animals," though, let's first imagine four different rooms.

Let's walk into a room full of Beavers. It's quiet but happy. Beavers don't require a lot of social interaction. Some Beavers will be talking quietly and seriously; others will be saying nothing at all; and some Beavers will have brought a book or laptop computer along to make the best use of their time. Beavers are content without a party.

Now come into a room full of Golden Retrievers. The noise level is higher here because these Golden Retrievers enjoy interacting so much. They are sharing, listening, and are very focused. They enjoy getting to know each other deeply.

If you dare, come into a room full of Otters. It's party time! In this room Otters are laughing, joking around, and clearly enjoying one another. Paper airplanes sail across the room and (look out!) someone brought a super-soaker. Otters love action and would rather not be alone. Otters feel responsible to help everyone have a good time.

Let's go now to the only room I hesitate to show you. It is the only unhappy room of the four. You see, Lions are uncomfortable until they figure out which of them is the main Lion. Until that is sorted out, there can be some terse exchanges, one-upmanship talk, and verbal sparring to see who gets the high ground.

It is not hard to see how these four personality types differ when it comes to job satisfaction. Lions are happiest when in charge of something or someone. They like to manage, give orders, and make decisions. Otters make great salespeople. Don't put an Otter behind a desk for long because she or he will long to be out with people. Golden Retrievers make great customer service representatives. You call up angry and they make you feel as if they've been waiting all day just to listen to your pain and inconvenience. I made just such a call about my Ford Taurus recently and the Golden Retriever on the other end listened to my pain, acknowledged my frustration, and kindly let me know they wouldn't do anything. When the conversation was over, I felt good about the call and Ford.

Beavers make great accountants, actuaries, and programmers. Facing a day of minimal human contact is no problem to them! It's energizing, not draining.

Getting the picture? Let's talk about love. Sociologists enjoy this stuff when it comes to attraction studies. Lion/Otter types tend to marry Golden Retriever/Beavers. It happens all the time. Lions find the sensitive Golden Retrievers so mysterious, so unfathomable, and so alluring. Golden Retrievers on the other hand are amazed at the confidence, direction, and outspokenness of Lions. Unfortunately, what is so mysterious and wonderful in the warm glow of pre-honeymoon attraction can be downright irritating a few years later.[3]

Do we find these animals in the Bible? No and yes. No, they are not listed along with the gifts of the Spirit. Yes, we certainly see personality differences in the Bible. Paul and Peter are very lion-like. Was Andrew an Otter? Friendship evangelism has been called *Operation Andrew* by the Billy Graham organization. How about Mary and Martha? Luke 10 reveals Martha as the organized Beaver and Mary as the soak-it-all-in Golden Retriever. I think Nehemiah was a combination Lion/Beaver. There's a combination that can get something done!

We've looked at these four personality tendencies from several different angles. Now let's make the leap to youth ministry. Who makes the "best" youth worker?

GOOD NEWS FOR ALL TYPES

It is encouraging to know that God uses all kinds of people in youth work. His calling is not limited to Lions only, or any one type. If we think about Jesus' selection of the Twelve, we are reminded that he chose a variety of personalities who would eventually be let loose to turn the world upside down.

Let's consider the strengths of each personality type as it pertains to expanding a youth ministry.

Lions have no hesitation about standing up in front of the troops. To lead a youth ministry someone has to be up there, right? If not a Lion adult, then a Lion kid can be comfortable being in charge. Many people fear speaking in front of others more than they fear death itself. Well, Lions don't have this problem. Lions are great at providing direction, vision, and a sense that this youth ministry is going places. They don't get bogged down with decision making. It would not take a Lion long to decide whether to do a mission trip, Operation Good News, or both.

On the other hand, I once overheard one end of a forty-five-minute phone conversation between two Golden Retrievers trying to decide what to do that same evening. It was clear that both wanted to be absolutely sure the other was happy and the other's needs were being met. Lions don't feel the need to prowl around the decision-making process like this. They say, "Let's decide and let's go!"

There is much in a Lion that is attractive to teenagers. Kids like a sense of purpose and direction. They want meaning. Lions are great when it comes to "telling it like it is" and leading youth into meaningful challenges, helping kids experience for themselves the joy of making a difference.

I have in front of me a 500-page text titled *The Sociology of Leisure*.[4] Well, Otters don't need a book to understand fun! Otters want to have a good time, but their desire is not selfish. They want others to have a good time as well. In youth work, Otters are the kind of people who make kids smile, laugh, and go home exclaiming "That was awesome!" Otters love to have fun, be it a spontaneous trip to Pizza Hut or a long-planned Jello-wrestling outreach event.

Otters make great youth workers because they want to make sure every single kid who walks in the door feels at least a little bit good. Otters work hard to create a positive atmosphere that attracts youths and makes them feel comfortable.

Kids are attracted to Otters because they're attracted to life. An Otter-led youth ministry is one in which youths feel good about the group and their involvement in it. They enjoy bringing friends because they know their friends will have a good time and hear a positive message.

Youth ministry is a job made in heaven for Golden Retrievers. Adolescence is a stormy time and it is rare when a kid doesn't feel insecure or hurting about something. Golden Retrievers are there for them! The gift of time and the gift of listening are blessings that a Golden Retriever brings to a youth ministry. They are concerned that the personal needs of young people be met.

Golden Retrievers are especially good at hanging out before and after a meeting or event. I have seen kids and Golden Retrievers standing around just talking in the parking lot long after the youth room is cleaned up, the lights are off, and the doors are locked.

Kids are attracted to Golden Retriever-led youth groups because they know they've got a friend. Programs do not bring people; people bring people. The connectedness kids feel to the Golden Retrievers in a youth ministry ensure their return again and again and again.

Beavers can also make great youth workers. Some kids are Beavers too and they can immediately sense when the leader is one of their own. Beavers are never sloppy in their organization of the youth ministry. Kids and parents know that if it appears on the youth calendar, it is going to happen and all details will be covered. The event, the ministry, is going to flow because the myriad of details needed to run a youth ministry are both understood and handled eagerly by Beavers. Beavers keep people informed, they don't lose money, and their word is good.

Beavers can be masters at one-to-one discipling, not only mentoring in spiritual truth, but also mentoring via modeling. I know Beaver youth workers who find kids to share their hobbies. Fishing, model boat building, and remote control aircraft flying are great arenas in which the Gospel can be nurtured in a young heart. Quality time is often a function of quantity time, and Beavers are very creative in finding areas where time can be invested in ministry.

Kids like Beavers because they like stability, trustworthiness, and excellence. Many appreciate the one-on-one emphasis which is all too absent in many homes.

In my survey, all types of personalities were associated with growing youth ministries:

YOUTH MINISTRY LEADERS		
Personality Type	Junior High	Senior High
Beaver	74%	48%
Golden Retriever	62%	54%
Otter	66%	59%
Lion	81%	69%

Each personality type drips with potential for expanding a youth ministry. Having said that, however, there is a downside to every upside. Our personalities, with all their God-given strengths, also have weaknesses as applied to youth ministry.

Lions are good at being insensitive, causing people to feel their opinions don't matter, and making rash decisions. Otters don't need anyone to disciple them about how to be disorganized, poorly prepared, or lacking in follow through. Golden Retrievers may appear nervous in front of twenty noisy junior highers. All the paperwork required to run a full-fledged youth ministry can seem like a crushing burden to them. Beavers won't attract many Otter youths since they find it difficult to project enthusiasm in the group setting.

In twenty-five years of being a youth worker, I've seen Lions get fired for being too stubborn. I've watched Otters pick up their last paycheck because their ministries did not have even a hint of structure or organization. I've seen tear-filled Golden Retrievers given the boot because they couldn't handle the size the youth group had grown to. I've observed Beavers sent packing because too many church kids complained that youth group was boring.

DON'T QUIT WORK—NETWORK

The key to overcoming the weaknesses inherent in our personalities is networking. First, we need to network with God. There is nothing like a glaring weakness that forces us to get on our knees and acknowledge that he is our source of strength, hope, and effectiveness. We have to trust God for the strength to function in the areas where we are weak.

Recently, one of my junior highers came to me and poured out a personal crisis. He was in pain and came to me for care. Internally I panicked, but as my spirit settled down, I was able to be used by God in this kid's life. I was weak, but in God's strength I was able to function.

You can bet your last Big Mac that this kind of spiritual exchange—human weakness for God's strength—takes place thousands of times across the country every week. Lions find themselves in counseling situations, Otters are writing up the summer camp reports for the governing board, Golden Retrievers are leading the "shuffle your buns" game, and Beavers are trying to keep fifteen wiggly junior highers from climbing out of the windows during Sunday school.

Networking with God is crucial; so is networking with others in youth ministry. In other words, we have to think "team." We need people who are not like ourselves to work alongside us in ministry. Lions especially need Golden Retrievers to provide the personal care youths so desperately need. Otters are in critical need of Beavers who can handle the details. Golden Retrievers need Otters and Lions who don't mind being in front of the group. Beavers need Otters to create the positive and fun atmosphere so essential to a growing youth ministry.

Sometimes we find ourselves functioning in areas where we are not strong, but we thank God for his grace and for the others who are filling out the whole personality picture with us.

There can be amazing joy in all of this. It is a joy to function in the areas of our strength. In one youth ministry I led, we had fifty adult volunteers. That's heaven for a Lion!

There is great joy in watching others in ministry as well. Recently, I had occasion to thank God for Golden Retriever Allison and how she puts her arms around those sixth-grade girls, making them feel so cared for. I thank God for Otter Mike, who tirelessly plays tag or basketball in the parking lot.

As we understand our God-given personalities, we are set free to serve him in enthusiastic joy.

We've looked at the big picture when it comes to youth group growth, at "growth anxiety," and at ourselves as well. Let's now look at our ministry. Church growth experts have identified certain numbers that can help us predict a lot about our attendance and potential for growth.

WHY GROUPS ARE GROWING

- "Ministering with a plan and a purpose." (Georgia, Lion)
- "We have fun. There's a short Bible talk before they go home." (Ohio, Otter)
- "The enthusiasm of the kids and their ownership in the ministry. We have a committed and visionary leadership team." (Michigan, Lion)
- Leaders are in contact with students on a weekly basis outside of our midweek meeting. We've reorganized the youth ministry concerning purpose and vision." (Alaska, Lion)

WHY GROUPS ARE NOT GROWING

- "Lack of organization on my part as youth minister." (Tennessee, Otter)
- "Bad, disorganized planning." (Kansas, Otter)

FOR WHAT IT'S WORTH

"We major on being purpose driven and goal oriented. Everything we do is targeted. Our Wednesday night gathering is for outreach. Our Sunday school and small groups are for growth. We're near a Christian college, so we were able to start an intern program and thus add staff." (California)

END NOTES

1. For a fascinating summary of the whole subject from a secular viewpoint see Winifred Gallagher's "How We Become What We Are" in *Atlantic Monthly* (Vol. 274, #3) September, 1994: 39ff.

2. See G. Smalley and J. Trent, *The Two Sides of Love* (Focus on the Family, 1990) and also Bob Phillips, *The Delicate Art of Dancing With Porcupines* (Ventura, Calif: Regal/Gospel Light, 1989).

3. While not using the same terms as Smalley, Trent, and Phillips, Jack and Carole Mayhall present a masterful guide to sailing these potentially troubled waters in marriage. See *Opposites Attract/Opposites Attack: Turning Your Differences Into Opportunities,* (Colorado Springs: NavPress, 1990).

4. John Kelly and Geoffry Godbey, *The Sociology of Leisure* (State College, Penn.: Venture, 1992).

4

TEFLON or VELCRO?

creating an attractive environment

I can still hear the mother's angry voice. "She doesn't like the group, Len. It's so cliquey, and no one reaches out to her. We had great hopes she would get involved but now we can't even force her to go. She has no friends in the group. We're thinking about leaving for a church with a better youth ministry." On that note, the conversation ended.

God knows what I wanted to say to that mother. Her ninth-grade daughter had not shown up more than twice during the six months she had been in the church. As I tossed and turned that night, I mentally gave Jana's angry mother a piece of my mind:

"Look, Mrs. Smith, we did everything we could to get Jana to come to the kickoff retreat in June. Kids called her. I called her. She said she wasn't interested. Since then we've called several times. The hostility in her voice reminds me of you. Do you remember when we sent a van full of kids over to your house to kidnap her and she refused to be kidnaped? And what about the special ninth-grade overnight we recently had—the best time to build relationships and feel connected? We have this retreat exactly for kids like Jana—but she went to the school dance instead. I think your daughter is a snobbish, thoroughly secularized pagan who has no desire to let God interfere with her fun. Sure, she'll blame us, but she's putting her time where her heart is. Don't tell me we haven't tried!"

Jana's family did leave the church (rather noisily, unfortunately) and joined another. I called that mom two years later to say hello and to see how things were going with Jana. Lo and behold, Jana was active in the new youth group, had rededicated her life to Christ, and had a wonderful Christian boyfriend in the group.

My feeling about Jana is different now than it was then. Experience has given me perspective on what happened with this family. As she surveyed the people in our group, the bottom line for Jana was that she couldn't see friendship potential.

Growing a healthy youth group means, among other things, creating a place where newcomers can stick, whether those newcomers are coming up through the ranks in the church (like Jana) or are coming from the outside. Sometimes we fail. It's discouraging to both kids and leaders to work hard inviting newcomers and see them stop coming after only a visit or two. Sometimes we succeed. It's exciting to lay awake at night thanking God for new kids who have come, met Christ, and become disciples.

What makes a ministry more like teflon or velcro has been studied by church growth specialists.[1] Much of their findings apply to youth ministry as well.

THE FRIENDSHIP FACTOR

The first crucial idea from church growth experts is this: newcomers must have at least seven friends in the church within their first six months or they won't stay. The friendship factor is even more vivid in youth ministry. Often, a new young person won't even show up to youth group unless they're coming with a friend. This friend serves as a bridge. In a healthy ministry, new friendships also happen as the new person starts coming regularly.

The question for us is, how do we help our kids be welcoming and open to new attenders? I've seen several methods work well:

- I hold the leadership core accountable for at least talking to new people. In our meetings, the questions regularly asked are, "Since we last met, whom have you spoken with in the group that you normally don't speak to? Whom of the new people have you spoken to?" It is easy for Lion and Otter young people to speak to newcomers but much less natural for Golden Retrievers and Beavers. It makes a tremendously positive impression on newcomers if their peers are friendly.
- I urge core leadership young people to invite newcomers to be part of their activities outside of youth group events. This is a big sign of social acceptance. A special problem often occurs when a guy brings a girl or visa versa. If a girl brings a guy, her friends will find it easy to speak with the newcomer, but generally other guys will steer clear. I urge our guys to not only speak to the new guy, but invite him to shoot hoops or play ping pong after youth group.
- Structuring for interaction provides chances for new kids to get a feel for who's there. In Chapter Two, we talked about the importance of small groups. As a new person is incorporated into a small group, he or she gets to know other peers as well as a caring adult leader.

We can pray, encourage, structure, and plan. Sometimes our newcomers will find ready acceptance and entrance. Other times things just won't click and they'll become an addition to the inactive portion of our mailing list. Our ministry may seem like a velcro group to some and a teflon group to others.

ROLL A ROLE

Having studied hundreds of churches, church growth specialists have concluded a church needs at least sixty roles or tasks for every one hundred attenders to be a growing church.

The ratio may not be exactly the same in youth ministry, but one thing we know for sure: kids like to feel that they are needed. They want to feel useful. Though youth will be content to sit and spectate for a while, they'll grow apathetic and invisible unless they have something to do. The importance of student involvement and ownership was mentioned repeatedly in the survey results.

You can provide your kids with meaningful involvement by utilizing the following suggestions.

Meaningful Roles for Youth

- *Cabinet*: a leadership core that meets twice monthly to pray, hold each other accountable, evaluate, and plan for the group.
- *Team Leaders*: students who are specially trained and provide care for teams of five to thirty within the larger youth group. They meet twice monthly for prayer, accountability, training, and planning for team caring, competition, and special team events. Examples of team caring include the following: birthdays; "missed you" cards or calls; celebration of academic, dramatic, music, or athletic successes; "secret pal" emphases; planned service projects in which the whole team gets involved.
- *Drama Team*: does skits for announcements, short sketches for themes in Bible study, and youth group theme presentations.
- *"Feel Good" Team*: a crack squad of Otters who will go to any lengths to make newcomers feel overwhelmed with friendship.
- *Graphics Team*: for artsy folk. They develop posters, flyers, and other printed publicity.
- *Multimedia Team*: in charge of taking slides or videos and making presentations at events.
- *Music Team*: selects and puts on before and after background music in the youth room, keeps cassette/CD lending library up-to-date and open on Sunday morning.
- *Worship Band*: in charge of live music at events or studies.
- *Youth Choir*
- *Quiz Team*: popular in some denominations, these kids memorize a large chunk of scripture during the year (the book of John, for example) and every six weeks go to quiz meets to compete against other groups.
- *Visitation Team*: load up the van, grab the chips and Mountain Dew, and show up at a missing student's home for a spontaneous party.

- *Mouthpiece Team*: practice and give up-front talks at youth group, share portions of the teaching load for midweek or Sunday school lessons.
- *Newspaper Team*: produce monthly publication for and about youth ministry members. Desktop publishing experts love this!
- *Adopt-a-Grandparent Team*: visits monthly with senior citizens.
- *Cooking Team*: meets monthly in church kitchen to bake cookies to give to active senior citizens in the church as a "thank you for your faithful service to the church."
- *Visiting-Cerebral-Palsy-Center Team*: a winner for kids who have the spiritual gift of mercy.
- *Letter-Writing Team*: to graduates away at college or in the military.
- *Service and Missions Teams*: over the years our groups have gone to Mexico, Bogotá, and Barcelona for missions; they have gone to Appalachia for house construction and Florida for hurricane cleanup.

Of course the list could be much longer than this. I've described briefly the ones with which I've had personal experience. But there are many more! If your group is large, you can do most or all of these simultaneously. If your group is smaller, start with the idea of a leadership core, then add other ideas one or two at a time.

GROUPS TO GROUP

The experts say we need at least seven smaller, relationally-centered groups for every one hundred persons who attend on Sunday morning and that at least two of these seven need to be fairly new—less than two years old. We may at first think this groups-to-group ratio doesn't apply to a small- or medium-size youth ministry, but it does. All of the groupings described in the previous section serve to support the relational infrastructure of a healthy youth ministry. The traditional Sunday school class also serves in this way (and also as a small group structure). The need for new relational groups arises because existing groups tend to plateau and become less able to assimilate new members.

This groups-to-group ratio is key to overcoming two common attendance plateaus.

GETTING FROM TEN TO TWENTY

Though sure to be a larger percentage if ALL church youth groups are considered, thirty percent of the junior high groups and twenty-eight percent of the senior high groups represented in the survey had an average of twelve or fewer students attending their main youth meeting. Twelve is the upper limit for a viable small group. There is a natural plateau here.

Normally, these youth groups get to the next level in two ways: congregational demographics bring an increasing tide of new junior highers to the shores of its youth ministry (the babies grow up), and/or the church itself grows, thus increasing the total pool of families with youths at the church.

If the above conditions don't exist, how can growth occur?

It is not a good idea to permanently split a group of 10 kids. They'll feel torn apart, isolated, and demoralized. The wise leader will begin to offer choices within this small group. For example, if a month of service projects is planned, two options can be offered which will both be positive. Half the group may want to bake in the church kitchen, and the other half may want to write letters to those who've graduated in the last three years. While a group of twelve is at a natural plateau, two dynamic groups of six are not. There is room for growth now—and don't be surprised if kids who didn't bring friends before now have a friend come along after this purposeful change to the normal program. Volunteer leadership is also a key; both groups should have a leader, not only to guide the group but to provide Christian relational care.

Don't ever return, then, to the "normal" program. Make sure there is always at least a brief opportunity for the small groups/teams/service groups to continue. Buttress this with an occasional you-must-bring-a-friend-to-come event, and pretty soon you'll get feedback from the senior highers that they don't feel comfortable bringing friends to events that include the wiggly and immature junior highers.

Now's the time to divide the group by age, assuming the leadership base can provide at least two adults per group. To mollify the eighth-grade girls (who want to be with senior high boys), promise a monthly joint meeting. Another way to defuse eighth-grade female angst is to grandfather them into part of the senior high program for the second half of the school year. For example, if they come to the Wednesday night junior high meeting they are free to come to the Sunday night senior high gathering. Remember also to emphasize kid ownership. The adults present are not necessarily there to plan and lead everything. Involve the troops at every level.

GETTING FROM THIRTY TO FORTY TO FIFTY-FIVE+
Churches ranging from 350 to one thousand have similar average atten-

dances at their youth group meetings *(see page 14)*. The smaller churches have around thirty junior and senior highers, and the churches two to three times their size average only around forty. This "fellowship barrier"[2] is explained by the fact that most people don't feel like they can really care about more than thirty to forty others. If a group is expected to be warm and fuzzy, it is almost guaranteed to remain below forty in attendance.

The key is developing a small group or team structure in which kids are not asked to care for the whole group but only for a specific subset. One group's pilgrimage to this kind of structure is described as a solution to school rivalry in Chapter Six. That group's attendance climbed from an average of thirty-five to an average of sixty in less than two months.

As in the transition from ten to twenty, the transition at this level is dependant on quality adult leadership that can provide sufficient care to make each young person feel connected.

Thus, healthy youth ministries are velcro youth ministries. They make it easy and even natural for newcomers to feel welcome and get connected.

Unfortunately, there are additional barriers to healthy growth. It doesn't take many obnoxious kids to throw a cold blanket on the hot fires of a growing youth group. What can you do about this?

WHY GROUPS ARE GROWING

- "The kids are on fire. They're bringing friends and they even organize and hold their own Sunday evening worship service. No adults allowed! It's great!" *(Iowa)*
- "Vision/mission/strategy within a targeted emphasis of student ministry. Students are excited about bringing others in." *(Indiana)*
- "Offering alternatives and meeting different needs with different programming." *(Ohio)*
- "Adding staff to adequately care for more kids." *(Indiana)*
- "Really working on developing relationships between adults and kids. Making each kid feel important and special just because they're them!" *(California)*

WHY GROUPS ARE NOT GROWING

- "Main kids all graduated." *(Texas)*
- "Older students have hard feelings about new leadership." *(Pennsylvania)*

FOR WHAT IT'S WORTH

"We have six basketball teams, a weight lifters club, a tae kwan do club, a worship-dance group, and a worship band. Our kids like to be involved!" *(New York)*

END NOTES

1. The ratios listed are from Win and Charles Arn, "Closing the Evangelistic Back Door," *Leadership* 5, no. 2 (Spring 1984): 22ff.

2. Lyle Schaller, "Why Forty Is a Fellowship Barrier," *Leadership* 5, no. 4 (Fall 1984): 48.

5

CHAPTER

PRACTICAL SOLUTIONS FOR SPECIFIC PROBLEMS

#1 obnoxious kids

We were nearing the end of my agenda for the cabinet meeting and it was about time to pray. As usual, I asked if there was anything else they wanted to talk about.

"Yah!" exclaimed Denny. "We need to talk about Dawn. She's ruining the group. I can't stand her and the reason some of my friends don't come any more is because she's there."

"That's right," added Andrea. "Dawn's a slut and everyone knows it. She shouldn't be allowed to come. Some of my friends say they're going to stop coming if she stays. I think she should be kicked out."

Matt quickly added, "I heard my parents talking about Dawn and they say a lot of the parents think she should be kicked out."

The other members of this junior high cabinet added similar comments. They were unanimous: Dawn had to go.

I could feel my usual optimism draining away like someone had pulled the plug on my soul. Here we were, finally reaching some formerly unreached kid (Dawn was dropped off weekly at youth group by a grandparent who felt we were her last hope), and what do my brightest and best kids do? Do they welcome her with open hearts and open arms, thanking God for the chance to be used in a new person's life? No, they go ballistic and start crusading for her removal.

I can't honestly remember what I said to the cabinet; I just remember being terribly discouraged. What were Dawn's crimes? She was boisterous, smelled like smoke, and swore.

I didn't kick Dawn out. Some kids quit coming, some parents complained, but I held my ground. When Dawn moved away a year later, there were not cheers but tears. Dawn had become a Christian, and her hard-shell, street-tough exterior had melted away to become one of the most enthusiastic, contagiously Christian kids I have ever seen. Her boisterous enthusiasm was now focused on God.

In the years since, I've known many teenagers who have managed to offend other youths by their very presence. As in the year Dawn started coming to junior high, I've seen attendance stall or decline as an apparent result.

So how can we remain faithful to our call to reach all kids for Christ while we try to keep the youth ministry healthy and growing? A key insight can help us stay sane when we have one or more unlovely young people in our youth group.

REMEMBER WHY THEY ARE SO RUDE

Abusive, odious, anti-social, rebellious, and uncooperative behavior can usually be pinned on one underlying cause: poor self-image. The kid who acts out negatively is sending out radar signals with the messages, "Notice me," "Respond to me," "Please tell me I'm somebody." One usually doesn't have to hire an espionage agent to understand why such signals are being sent out. Here are five faces that instantly come to my mind and the easy-to-discuss sources of their dysfunctions:

Dawn (nonchurched background): Broken home. Father, a fashion designer commuting between LA and New York spoke to her, at best, twice a year. Mother, whenever Dawn would run away from Grandma's and come "home," would summarily kick her out and order her not to come back.

Jason (strong Christian parents, core church family): Father off-the-charts passive-aggressive, an expert at finding the thunderstorm in every silver cloud, holding an advanced degree in Communicating My Wishes through Screaming.

Roberta (nonchurched background): Broken home, rejected by both parents, bounced between relatives or living on the street.

William (Christian parents, active in church): Sullen, uncommunicative father who seems absolutely incapable of saying the words, "love" or "good job."

Jeanne (Christian parents, core church family): Both Mom and Dad very perfectionistic, viewed as everyone's ideal of good Christian parents. At church whenever the doors opened. Parents inadvertently communicated to Jeanne, though, that she was never quite good enough for them or for God.

If your mind is flipping through the sad or angry faces of kids you have known, you are probably also seeing in their backgrounds indicators why this guy or that girl was acting the way they were.

There is a plethora of books and curricula on the subject of self-image and how to help kids with it. Though it may have taken a lifetime for the obnoxious kid to become that way, it may not take long to see improvement if we are capable of showing love and acceptance in a way that registers. I have found four responses to be effective in working with unlovely kids:

RESPONSE #1: CHRISTIAN RELATIONAL CARE

This term, coined by British youth leader Pete Ward, refers to the constellation of things we do that show Christ's love to youths. We could launch into an exposition of the Beatitudes, the fruit of the Spirit, or Jesus with the woman at the well, but most of us have a picture in our heads of what it means to show love to young people in a Christlike way. We listen, we show interest in their interests, we don't appear shocked when they come to youth group with green hair and a nose ring. We call them on the phone, invite them to help us on projects, and affirm the good in them. If they reject us continually, we appear unfazed continually. We face this rejection with the inner assurance that though they may hate us now, it's almost certain that in the future they will realize the fortress they have erected to protect them from pain is actually made of sand. Eventually they will wonder if there is any rock to stand on. Then it will hit them: "You know, that youth pastor . . . maybe she has it right after all."

As we love kids, we also encourage other adults to similarly accept and love them.

RESPONSE #2: A WELL-FED CORE

We've already spoken about the importance of having a leadership core in youth ministry. Even a core of two to three kids can exert a powerful influence when it comes to dealing with rude and obnoxious peers.

Over the years I have learned how to help this core have a heart for the unlovable. I've usually had a pending school year's leadership in place by June. We have an orientation meeting the month before people disappear for the summer. In this meeting, I include the following:

"I'm so glad and thankful you have agreed to serve on this leadership team. I thought it would be encouraging to have each of us here tell the others why you are willing to help the group by serving in this way. Why are you willing to be in this leadership core?"

The answers I hear in response to this question are along these lines:

■ "I want to see the group grow and new people come to Christ."
■ "I want the group to be more unified, loving, and caring."
■ "I want to see us do fun stuff."

I affirm each of these responses, then add a follow-up question:

"Do you mean you want the group to grow with people just like us, and to be loving and unified with people just like us, and be even more fun for people just like us, or do you mean there is room here for people who may be different, even those who are not yet Christians?"

No one has ever responded, "Yes Len, we mean to exclude those kinds of people. We're a nice country club here; that's what we want." All affirm they are open to the unlovely.

You can instantly see how helpful this is when someone does start to come who is obnoxious. If the cabinet that was in place the year Dawn came on the scene had experienced a healthy orientation, their response may have been quite different. If the leadership group has temporary amnesia about their original commitment, it doesn't take much to jog their memory. When we are all back on the same page, I then say, "My guess is that people who are like ____ usually don't feel very good about themselves. What can we do to try to help ____ feel cared for here?" After ideas are shared, we make individual specific commitments, duly noted in our leadership notebooks, to which we are agreeing to be held accountable and about which we will report at our next meeting in two weeks.

These specific commitments can include:

- "I'll call her this week and invite her to the progressive dinner."
- "I'll make sure I talk to him next time he comes."
- "I'll talk to Paula and Cheryl the next time they gossip about her and ask them to stop."
- "I'm going to pray every day that he'll become a Christian real soon."

RESPONSE #3: APPROPRIATE DISCIPLINE

Jill, Kenora, and Lisa managed to disrupt their junior high Sunday school class not just every week, but about every 10 minutes. It wasn't only talking or being boisterous; their misbehavior involved poking the kids around them and hitting whatever wall they happened to be close to with their heads, knees, feet, or elbows. After class, they ganged up on the younger girls (and boys) and tried to pick fights.

Jill was from a core church family, Kenora was Jill's non-Christian friend, and Lisa was Kenora's friend (who was on her third school that year, having been expelled from the previous two). I began to receive a torrent of bad news about the class—from the teacher, the other kids, and parents. Attendance declined. I started hearing, "No way will I invite a friend with these jerks here."

After appropriate warnings of consequences that were laughed off with a shrug, we did what we had to do. I informed the three of them:

- They were removed from Sunday school until fall.
- I had found a leader who was willing to have a class just for them, if they wanted it.
- They had forfeited the privilege of going to our summer camp.

It was the third of these three that brought weeping, wailing, and gnashing of teeth. Apparently they had already been planning a camp experience that would be memorable in various illegal and immoral ways. While Lisa had no parents that could be found (she lived in a succession of foster homes), I did inform Jill and Kenora's parents of the decision. Jill's parents were deeply shamed by their daughter and believed the step was necessary. Kenora's father, though living in a different state, got word to us that he was impressed that the church seemed to have standards.

When a kid's behavior is severe enough to result in the kind of reaction described, appropriate consequences should be articulated and enforced.[1]

RESPONSE #4: STUDENT SELF-SORTING

One of the most productive and positive steps we can take in response to unruly youth group members is to give the kids a chance to sort themselves. Read on if you're having trouble picturing this.

The most important change I made during fourteen years of ministry in Seattle was the institution of a "First Half/Second Half" format for the Wednesday night senior high ministry. First Half was fun, fast moving, light, and the Bible talk was definitely given with non-Christians or less-than-enthusiastic listeners in mind. Then we took a ten-minute refreshment break. It was what happened after this break that was so radical.

During Second Half, kids had three choices: they could go home, hang out around the pool table or in the parking lot, or, attend Second Half, which was for worship, deeper Bible study, and prayer. (Job survival note: Before I implemented First Half/Second Half, I got the approval of the Christian education committee and parents. Also, the cabinet knew all about it and were expected to be at Second Half.)

After we made the change, there was an amazing sense that God was showing up at youth group during Second Half. That sense of presence and power became so real that it wasn't long before eighty percent of the group chose to attend Second Half.

Sunday school is another arena for student self sorting. One quarter, I offered three electives: *Tension Getters* (a role-playing curriculum from Youth Specialties), an introduction to C.S. Lewis (complete with homework and in-class presentations), and a nursing home ministry (during which they went to a facility just six blocks from the church).

Of the twenty-five kids who normally showed up for Sunday school, the rowdies actually liked Tension Getters. It was led by a quintessential Otter and they all had great fun. Those that signed up for C.S. Lewis were thrilled to able to be serious without the mocking of the rowdies. In the nursing home, my quietest and most apathetic kids woke up. They felt useful!

WHY GROUPS ARE GROWING

- "We have finally gotten a reputation at the junior high school for being a fun, warm place to be." *(Manitoba)*
- "Small group training, especially for student leaders. Group goals established by them." *(Maryland)*
- "Switch to a relational ministry. I focus on our students as a volunteer for ten to fifteen hours a week. I get to avoid the office politics and take care of students." *(California)*
- "We've changed the program more toward small groups." *(Minnesota)*

WHY GROUPS ARE NOT GROWING

- "Our kids just don't like the other kids they're with." *(Illinois)*
- "Since we have a combined junior/senior high youth group, the older ones stopped coming because they don't want to be around the junior highers." *(Pennsylvania)*

FOR WHAT IT'S WORTH

"I try to steal like a bandit the good ideas I get from other groups. But mainly we focus on communicating personal care to kids. We can't compete with the glitz of sports and concerts, but we can offer relationships and being there for them.

"I try to remember that in other settings, these relationships aren't available. Sure, their teachers or coaches may care about them, but the ratios are too high—too many kids for each adult.

"In our group we offer what they can't get elsewhere." *(Washington)*

END NOTES

1. For a thorough treatment of this important subect see Les Christie, *How to Work with Rude, Obnoxious and Apathetic Kids* (Wheaton, Victor Press, 1994), which deals with youth group discipline. My own book, *Teen Shaping* (Revell, 1991), is a guide for parents about discipline in their home setting.

6

PRACTICAL SOLUTIONS FOR SPECIFIC PROBLEMS

#2 *rivalries*

I was having one of those nights with our junior high group where everything went right. Well, almost everything.

Attendance was good and the games went well. The kids participated with enthusiasm and did not cop an "I'm too cool for this" attitude. They sat quietly during my talk and their body language betrayed them—they were actually interested. When I asked a question for discussion, many hands shot up. (I told you it was a good night!) My theme was unity and being kind to one another. I waxed eloquent that our youth group, diverse as it is, needs to be a safe place where we can come and not feel put down. "We all hunger for our group to be this safe place." Thirty-five early adolescent heads nodded their assent. It was one of those times when, had it been a camp situation, we would have joined hands around the campfire and sung "Kumbaya" with faces and hearts aglow.

"Let's close in prayer, and I hope many of you will lead us in praying about this issue." And pray they did. The sentence prayers were like popcorn bursting all over the room. Even some of the guys prayed out loud (a rarity for us). You may be thinking this story is too good to be true, but believe me, it was one of those nights where things went right. Right, that is, until just after my last "amen."

Sitting on my left side were "the men." These guys try to act tough, macho, and oh-so-cool. The girls were on my right. To the delight of his friends, Troy yelled, "Hey Jenny, you're fat and ugly!" He rolled over in laughter and was joined by several of the other guys in uproarious delight at such a well-timed insult. While the guys were still rolling on the floor, Jenny stood to her feet, briefly surveyed the guys who were mocking her, burst into tears, and ran from the room, followed by her friends. Had these girls been armed, the looks they gave as they left to find Jenny indicated the morning headline in the Nyack Journal would have been "Mass Slaying at Church Youth Group."

The rest of the group quickly dispersed as parents arrived to pick up their kids. It didn't take a Ph.D. to speculate what would be reported to parents on the way home.

Of course, I confronted Troy. He was one of the guys who had just prayed so fervently for unity in our group! He blew me off without remorse, saying, "She's just my sister. I can say what I want!"

TOE TO TOE

Rivalries—sibling, interpersonal, male versus female, school versus school—can all quickly lay waste to our carefully and prayerfully laid plans for a warm, accepting, and growing youth ministry.

I've seen it all when it comes to rivalry's cruel work. I've learned two things: to understand rivalry when I see it, and to proactively prevent it whenever possible.

Rivalry is part of adolescent behavior. It is normal, it will happen, and woe to the youth worker who thinks his or her kids are not capable of amazingly cruel actions toward their Christian peers. Knowing that it is normal (if despicable) helps me to be grateful for the times when rivalry does not rear its ugly head.

One guy in my group has a Jekyll-and-Hyde personality. Some Wednesday nights he is cooperative, supportive, likeable, and sociable. Other Wednesday nights, he verbally abuses all who come within five feet of him. He starts at least one fight on his bad nights. Driving to church, I always wonder, "What will Big Man be like tonight?"

Without a doubt, there is one thing that has helped me keep kids like Big Man and Troy from causing me to abandon youth work. Big Man, Troy, and kids like them cannot yet "think about a thought."

If you've ever taken an adolescent psychology class, you've heard the name of Jean Piaget (pronounced Pee-ah-ZHAY). He studied children and teenagers and made the observation that mental development does not happen smoothly over time. The mental and emotional maturation graph looks more like a staircase than an incline. That's just another way of saying that kids' brains are wired up at a certain approximate age, and this wiring then enables them to function at a certain level. Things are then on hold for a year or three until the next cerebral upgrade takes place.

Parents of small children know that at first, when you hide a ball behind a box, the child thinks it's gone. He or she makes no attempt to find or search for it. The ball has vanished from sight and also from the mind of the child. A year later, after mental rewiring takes place, that same child will know the ball is behind the box and take deliberate action to get it. This growth is a marvel to watch in children as well as in teenagers. Fortunately for us, it can have everything to do with staying sane when rivalry in any of its ugly forms appears in our youth group.

The upgrade that most applies to teenagers is what Piaget called "formal operations" or what I call "second-order consequences/second-order connections." This occurs between ages eleven and thirteen for girls and the ages of thirteen and eighteen for boys.

Nine-year-olds don't make very good chess players. They can easily grasp the moves each player can make, but they have real difficulty envisioning a strategy involving a series of moves. Sixteen-year-olds can do this pretty well and, with practice, embark on a battle plan several moves in the making, envisioning the likely outcomes of each move as well as potential responses to opponent moves.

This has everything to do with Troy and Big Man. Troy sincerely loves the Lord and can easily and willingly pray in response to a talk on group unity and kindness. Unfortunately the cerebral upgrade has not taken place in his head yet, so there is quite literally no connection between "Christians are nice to people," "I am a Christian," and "Therefore I should be kind to others, even my sister." It is especially the "therefore" that is a particular mystery to Troy's brain. It does not compute, it has no meaning, and like the ball behind the box for a one-year-old, it's just not there. The good news is that I've watched Troy enough to know that he is probably within twelve months of a whole new world of mental possibilities. And this new world will eventually include the "therefore" we've just discussed.

Big Man is the same age chronologically as Troy, but not mentally. As with Troy, the linkages connecting "Christians show the fruit of the Spirit," "I'm a Christian," and "Therefore I should be nice to people when I come on Wednesdays" just aren't there. Again, it's the "therefore" that is missing. I'd say he's two to four years away from the lights coming on. In the meantime, he'll continue to be a saint one week and a terror the next.

The girls in our junior high ministry, virtually all of whom have long been capable of this abstract reasoning, are scandalized by the actions of Troy and Big Man. Junior high male stupidity, cruelty, insensitivity, and immaturity are mind boggling to them. They see the boys as quintessential examples of the statement, "The lights are on but no one is home."

I am not saying that pre-abstract reasoning boys are not capable of being growing Christians. I am saying that spiritual growth will become much more conspicuous as the mental transitions take place.

Another outworking of a kid who has moved to this new mental level is the ability to put himself or herself in another person's shoes. Empathy is the term, and the absence of empathy in a developing teen virtually guarantees at least occasional non-Christian behavior.

All this helps me stay sane because I know most of my obnoxious junior high boys will be spiritual giants a few years down the line. Right now, they are mentally challenged. I don't love, enjoy, or appreciate Troy any less because of the cruel way he treated his sister. Similarly, I wouldn't think poorly of a quadriplegic just because he or she couldn't play basketball. God is the one who wired our brains to develop as they do, and by his grace, gives youth workers the patience to hang in there as kids mature.

I confront Troy and Big Man when they say or do something clearly wrong. I sometimes give them a "time out" or other discipline. Occasionally they are even remorseful. I just know they are not yet capable of making a promise for improvement that will hold for more than twenty minutes at a time.

This insight helps us understand sibling and some forms of interpersonal rivalries within the group. There are other forms of rivalry that can also spoil the warm and friendly atmosphere we so desperately want to develop.

SCHOOL RIVALRIES

One youth ministry I led included teenagers from twenty-six different high schools. It could be tense in the group when our two main schools were about to face off in a big sports contest. It never, however, blew up in our faces. It never became a hindrance to growth. Many were astounded that such a diverse group could be so accepting and feel so close.

How did we achieve this harmony? Two proactive steps we took kept the lid on the destructive potential of school rivalries.

First, our teams brought unity at a small group level. Our group had five teams, each with about twenty-five names on its roster and ten to fifteen who showed up regularly on Wednesday nights. To assemble the teams, I asked each student to put on a card the names of two to four friends that They Must Not Be Separated From Under Any Circumstances. We use to call these cliques, but now enlightened youth workers call them "friendship clusters." Trying to balance guys/girls and regular attenders/infrequent attenders put five to seven friendship clusters on a team.

As friendship clusters nudged up against one another in the context of the team, cross-friendship cluster communication would take place. Over time, it even resulted in something looking like unity.

Teams met in several different settings. During a typical Sunday school hour, they met in teams for the final fifteen to twenty minutes to discuss an aspect of the lesson or work on a project (for example, developing a skit illustrating patience). On Wednesday nights, the teams assembled first. During these ten minutes, new kids were introduced and welcomed and a quick "How are you?" was led by one of the three adults in charge of each team. They also got ready for the subsequent team competition game. The game sometimes involved only one or two representatives of the team; sometimes the whole team was involved. It varied from week to week.

About forty-five minutes later we began Second Half (see page 52), the serious part involving worship singing, more discussion about the Bible talk from First Half, and time in teams again. This final team gathering for the evening included prayer, support, and accountability.

Each team had three kids serving as team leaders and three adult facilitators. Occasionally a team would hold a dinner, go on a special outing, work together on a service project, or plan an overnight.

It isn't hard to see why this reduced school rivalries. Everyone who was involved in the youth ministry was solidly connected to a team. The team included their best friends and people from other schools with whom they had become acquainted as the year went on. When it came time for their school's big game, I was astounded at how often kids from a particular youth group team would sit together in the bleachers while their opposing school football teams pounded each other on the gridiron.

Our leadership core set the tone for the group. We had twelve kids who served on the cabinet. They were in charge of all planning for the group and other major decisions. We met together for two hours every other week. We prayed for each other, held each other accountable, and made decisions about the group. The meeting always ended the same way. We got on our knees in a circle and prayed, not for each other, but for the youth group.

After one has logged enough "knee time," things like school rivalries seem trivial. The leadership core modeled support and unity. They were spread out evenly on the teams, and it was clear that there were people in this youth ministry who cared.

I had the chance to test the transferability of these ideas when I moved across the country to take a different youth ministry position. I moved into a group that was, shall we say, dysfunctional. One of my early goals was to have members not swear at each other in anger before, after, and during youth events.

After a year of cabinet, First Half/Second Half and teams, the tone of the group had changed radically. It started to grow numerically as well.

GUY/GIRL BREAKUPS

No matter what the size of the youth ministry, adolescent love gone bitter can destroy the atmosphere of a youth group. Not only the former couple is involved—their friends take sides, things are said, things are said by people who heard things said, and the whole group is soon consumed by gossip and rivalry.

I remember the week after an especially messy guy/girl breakup. My senior pastor smilingly introduced me to a new family visiting the church. "Len, why don't you take John and Karla with you to the youth meeting and introduce them around." Being a good youth worker, when my senior pastor said, "Jump," I asked, "How high?" But that morning, I wanted to say, "No. Oh please no, not now. Everyone hates each other down there." I prayed silently while leading those two new nervous teenagers down the stairs to the youth room, "Lord, we need a miracle here, pleazzzzzzzz!"

While not guaranteed miracle makers, there are two ways I've learned to cope with breakup fallout.

First, when young love blossoms, I speak with the new couple. Couples often attend more after the onset of their coupledom than previously, since it gives them more time to be together. With appropriate personal modifications, I have a little fireside chat with Mr. and Ms. In-Love that goes like this:

"Hey, Romeo and Juliet, I see you both have great taste! Congratulations on going out. I think it's great, and I'm glad we've got lots of stuff you can come to and be at together. There are a couple of things I'd like to mention.

It's really important that you not hang all over each other when you're at youth group because it makes people, especially new people, uncomfortable. Please don't lose your care for others here, because they need you. It's fine to be together, but don't forget everyone else. Another thing, as you know, I do weddings. But in all the weddings I've done, only one or two have been with people who went together during high school. So, there is a slight chance that your relationship may grow apart before you graduate. Could you decide, even now, that if your relationship ends, that you'll do so maturely—still as friends and appreciating what God has given each of you? It's a big deal, because you can probably remember when the youth group iced over because _____ and ____ broke up and it was such a mess. Anyway, I know it seems funny to think about breaking up now, but I know you are both mature. A friendly parting is an incredible sign of maturity. And say, if you stay together, I'll do that wedding down the line, okay?"

Second, I do a lot of spiritual warfare praying. Satan doesn't want our ministries to be successful; he'll try anything to mess up group unity. I talk about this with the cabinet and we pray. When I feel we're in a time of particular spiritual warfare, I call ten friends and ask them to pray. Prayer cover is vital for a youth ministry that wants to see God work and to see new people come.

We've talked about rivalries. Now, what do we do when the hindrance to a growing youth ministry is not rivalries or obnoxious kids, but a lack of the precious commodity called space?

WHY GROUPS ARE GROWING
- "We're allowing the kids to run the show." *(Ohio)*
- "Implementing an outreach/inreach ministry." *(Arizona)*
- "Patience, faith, and joint leadership between youth and adults." *(Texas)*

WHY GROUPS ARE NOT GROWING
- "Senior girls who constantly put down the younger girls. Our ninth and tenth grade girls refuse to bring friends because of this." *(New Jersey)*
- "I've been here a long time and some years seem to go better than others. We're in a down time now. The kids we have don't have anything in common. There is no chemistry making the group a group." *(California)*

FOR WHAT IT'S WORTH
"We started a street hockey time every day after school in the church parking lot for junior highers and it worked. Kids came regularly and started to come to our Friday night outreach events. We also designated one room in the church as the Studio by getting some decent sound and recording equipment. This attracted other kids." *(New Jersey)*

7

CHAPTER

PRACTICAL SOLUTIONS FOR SPECIFIC PROBLEMS

#3 lack of space

I felt sad and mad. I wanted to say "I told you so" to any member of our esteemed property committee that I could find. The youth group had been growing. We had passed the "Eighty Percent Equals Full" rule and broken the forty barrier for two consecutive weeks. I could see we didn't even have a prayer for continued growth unless we could get out of the youth room. Unfortunately, all the other existing rooms were smaller. To make room for growth, we would need to move into the gym. The youth staff and I had agreed it was our only choice. Our plan was that each week we would lift the couches out of the youth room, roll up the carpet, and recreate our room in one end of the gym: carpet, sofas, video, sound system, bulletin boards, everything. With the space dividers we could roll into place it would still have the living-room feel we wanted.

We were all set. Set, that is, until the chairman of the property committee informed me that our plans were not acceptable. They had just spent $50,000 on a new gym floor. It was a state-of-the-art floor for basketball, floor hockey, volleyball, church banquets and other church meetings. But woe be to us if we moved a couch out onto that floor. A carried couch could be a dropped couch. "The risk is just too great, Len."

The next Wednesday, we had fifty kids and eight adult staff jammed in our room. Some came late and stood outside the door because there was literally "no room in the inn." I said to myself, "Well, I'm seeing the high water mark of this youth group, at least for now, anyway." Attendance dropped by ten, and then five. Attendance thus sank until the group size was about eighty percent of the room's actual capacity.

NO-ROOM BLUES

You may not have experienced my exact situation, but you may have experienced similar space-related problems that can prove so frustrating to our vision for a growing ministry.

When confronted by a lack of space, the first and best alternative is to find or build a better and larger facility. One church I served took this to heart and replaced a fifteen-by-twenty-foot multipurpose youth room with a truly Cadillac senior high-only room of four thousand square feet, nicely carpeted, and complete with fireplace. If the senior high group didn't grow, I could no longer blame it on lack of space, that's for sure!

We'll consider the idea of proposing a building addition at the end of this chapter. Short of the new-construction ideal, there are three viable alternatives we can explore when confronted with lack of space.

ACCESS MORE SPACE (IF YOU DARE)

Relocating to a larger room in the church can require the wisdom of Solomon and the political skills of an ambassador. Unfortunately, turf wars over space are not uncommon in churches. When negotiating for bigger and better space in your current church building, remember these tips:

- Never assume you can just move in and occupy a new space.
- Share with your pastor, CE committee, or other relevant governing authority the excitement of a growing youth ministry, the need to have more room soon. Then solicit ideas for resolving this happy problem. (Eventually you'll be asked for your opinion.)
- Be profuse in your appreciation if some organization or group in your church voluntarily gives up space so that the youth ministry can grow.

If you are given space that will be primarily yours, be thankful! More likely, you will be given new space that is also used by another group at another time. If you are not allowed to personalize the room with posters, carpet, sofas, etc., you can still prepare portable bulletin boards and make places for posters, pictures of youth group members, pictures from the last retreat or big event, and announcements about upcoming events. Unroll a small carpet, add a portable ping pong table and boom box, and behold—a youth room is born.

THE TIMES, THEY ARE A CHANGIN'

Are you looking at the above ideas and thinking, "Been there, done that," or "None of the above"? Consider changing the time when your youth ministry meets.

Many churches have midweek Family Night when families come, then split up for various activities. (Don't ask me why this is called Family Night.) The result of such programming is often overcrowded facilities on that one night.

Go to the powers that be and request the youth group be unhinged from Family Night. Be enthusiastic about the growth you are seeing. The fact that there needs to be a change should be seen as an exciting problem. Moving the youth ministry away from the Family Night slot will permit other groups meeting on that night to expand into your space. It is a potential win-win situation.

Don't go to the higher ups until you've first met with parents. They'll need to be convinced of the problem and willing to support the solution. If youth ministry members don't live in close proximity to the church building, car or van pools may need to be part of the proposal. Most parents are tired when coming home from work and the thought of another night out transporting kids around is not appealing. A well-thought-out car pooling plan can make the difference in parental attitudes.

DIVIDE AND CONQUER

Still another way to make room for numerical growth is to split up or decentralize the youth group. You can split the senior high from the junior high, or the college from the senior high. A divide-and-conquer plan can make great sense on paper, but extreme care must be taken in implementing such a plan. I made a huge mistake in this regard early in my ministry.

It was my first month in my first church after seminary, and I succeeded in expertly alienating a huge number of people. I managed to create such a personal relations disaster that it took two years for some people to accept me. One family even left the church over my faux pas.

In this new church, I was to be in charge of the junior high, young peoples' (high school and college combined) group, and young couples' groups. I had it in the back of my mind that it would be nice to eventually split off the college kids from the high schoolers. It seemed to me that twenty-four-year-olds and fifteen-year-olds were light years apart when it came to needs. Also, the group was large (over fifty) and splitting it would make each group more manageable. On the last day of my candidating weekend, the search committee asked what I felt their needs were. I mentioned that I thought an eventual separation of the high school/college group would be wise. They agreed, and I didn't give the matter a second thought.

On my second Sunday after arriving, the church education director told me there was a group of people I needed to meet with. I naively agreed and went to the meeting. Pastor Bob had gathered eight twenty-four-year-olds with whom he had talked about my plans to split the group. They were very much in favor of the split. Furthermore, they wanted it now.

"I was thinking maybe a big change like that would be good a year down the line, but wow, if there is this much grassroots support, let's go for it!" I responded.

Later, I made our intentions widely known. It was one of the dumbest things I've ever done.

The announcement unleashed a fire storm of protest and disapproval. Kids yelled at me. Parents phoned me in tears. All of a sudden my name was mud.

Why all the angst? You guessed it. The high school girls were absolutely, totally, and unalterably opposed. I quickly learned the bottom line: High school girls want to be with college men, not boys their own age. Upset this social configuration and judgment day quickly cometh.

Now I was in a lose-lose . . . high school girls screaming at me and twenty-two to twenty-five-year-olds reminding me that I had promised them the change would be made. The status quo and the proposed change were both unacceptable to someone. I chose to proceed with the change and ride out the storm. The result was that the college group got off to a strong start and the high school group that was left (after most girls boycotted) limped along until a huge group of junior highers graduated to make the group viable again. It was a miserable five months.

It would have helped if I would have:
■ Not promised change to anyone so soon.
■ Solicited feedback from the senior highers and their parents before making any decisions.
■ Highlighted the benefits to the senior highers (leadership development, numerical growth potential, ease of transporting the group to multi-church high school events, meeting their needs, etc.).
■ Insisted that the decision not be mine, but the Christian education committee's or the church council's.
■ Instituted the change slowly, grandfathering current senior highers—if a senior higher attended the functions of the senior high group, he or she was also welcome at the college events.

A group split will create space for future growth. A church that is planting a daughter church is a parallel example. In one such church-mothering experience in Seattle, we sent off over one hundred people to begin the new work. On the following Sunday, our senior pastor prayed, "Thank you, Lord for the empty pews we see today and the opportunity they represent." Empty space in our youth room may similarly present us with new opportunity for growth.

Another way to divide and conquer is to decentralize the youth ministry. If you're crowded in one location at the church building and have no on-site options, meet in two or more homes instead. True, a home may not be suitable for programming that involves pudding fights or large-group games. Yet there is much to be gained from this approach. Intimacy and accountability are more easily attained in a group of ten to thirty than forty or more. Youth ministries taking this approach usually divide by schools so that each of the major schools represented has a designated home meeting in its own area. Kids who are from under-represented schools or who are home schooled can be folded into one of the larger groups or have a special group comprised of individuals like themselves.

Try to meet as an entire group at least monthly. You may need to use the church sanctuary or fellowship hall. In that setting, everyone can enjoy the large group games, singing, and other activities that make a large group so exciting.

You can assure the success of a decentralized approach by developing and nurturing quality adult leaders. Meet with leaders weekly to evaluate, troubleshoot, plan, and pray. Maintain good communication with host homes. Be fanatical about cleanup and expressions of appreciation.

To make decentralization work you might consider producing a youth group newsletter including features and reports from the different groups. A group that is especially bonded may want to take on a service project like sponsoring a needy child or visiting a retirement home. If you still have a youth room, give each home group space on a bulletin board. Bulletin board items can include maps to host homes, pictures of group members, and pictures of special service projects or other activities (like toilet papering the senior pastor's home).

LIGHT AT THE END OF THE TUNNEL

Problems related to space are vexing. I've slated Sunday school classes to meet in bathrooms, closets, hallways, buses, restaurants, nearby homes, and the church kitchen. Kids are flexible. Led with a sense of humor and a dash of creativity, even some of the most unlikely spaces can be salvageable. The church kitchen is one of my favorite unlikely places for youth Sunday school. Whenever that has been my lot (and it has been many times over the years), I always produce a schedule of who's bringing food. Sometimes we've cooked up a nice hot breakfast with different aspects of the meal delegated to different kids. This breaks the ice and helps kids feel comfortable.

WHEN IT'S TIME TO BUILD

All creativity aside, however, the space solutions just listed are much more bearable if there is a plan, even a distant one, that will provide a long-term solution to your problem. If it's the right time to try to get a building program approved by your church keep the following ideas in mind:

■ Schedule your adult groups to meet for at least one Sunday in the spaces the youth normally use. Holding the women's Bible study in the broom closet, the Homebuilders in the bathroom, and the men's Bible study strung out along Hall B will help adults get the picture.

■ Get parents concerned. Take parents on a guided tour of the facilities your group now uses. See how many will fit in the ladies' restroom.

■ Make sure your kids are visible to the congregation. Schedule them to read scripture or pray in the morning service. Have your cabinet visit and lead the midweek prayer service regularly. If you have an evening service, let the youth group plan and lead it quarterly. Have your youth leadership agree to sit in the front of the sanctuary during worship.

■ During a building program, have the youth hold a "thank you" banquet for the church. You can schedule a lock-in and make part of the Saturday schedule include actually working on the building or cleaning up construction mess. Challenge your youth to give financially and assist them in raising money for the new building.

A POSITIVE PROBLEM

Being out of space is a decidedly positive problem. It means our ministries are growing and have great potential for further growth. Yet, no matter what the size of our ministries, we should be able to enjoy what we have. Even in nongrowing situations, it helps to see the good. In the next chapter we'll take a look at how we can do that.

WHY GROUPS ARE GROWING

■ "We try very hard to show individual care. We do birthday cards, show up at school events, write notes of appreciation, and call friends. Unconditional acceptance is the key." *(Kentucky)*

■ "Our small groups make a big difference for us. They do fun stuff in the large group, but in small groups they grow in prayer, their relationships with God, and their relationships with each other." *(New Mexico)*

WHY GROUPS ARE NOT GROWING

■ "Our church has no vision for youth ministry. The rooms they give us are ugly and they won't let us fix them up." *(Pennsylvania)*

■ "We should divide the group, but the rest of the spaces in the building are used by children's activities that night. We have the space to expand into, but the parents are against switching nights." *(Indiana)*

FOR WHAT IT'S WORTH

■ "We are totally purpose driven. Everything in this junior high ministry has a focus. Our Bible study time is called Herd and our small groups are called Graze Groups. We have Stampede as a monthly outreach night. The kids love it and bring lots of friends." *(Nebraska)*

8

ENJOYING WHAT YOU HAVE

"**W**ell Lord," I prayed silently, "it's not exactly as I thought it would be, but I want to get over this setback. Please let me just enjoy these kids." I looked again at the eighty-foot marble waterfall that is the visual centerpiece of the Trump Tower Atrium in midtown Manhattan. It was a beautiful sight, except for one small item—the waterfall was dry.

It was June. I had arrived at a church located outside of New York City in February. Not being a great fan of graduation banquets, but not wanting to abandon cherished tradition, I convinced the banquet committee that we should do something different for dessert. "Let's charter a nice bus, and after the program, head into the city. I think we can get Trump Tower just for our use." I extolled the virtues of the place, and made a big deal of how great it would be to eat dessert in the Marble Terrace Cafe at the base of the spectacular indoor waterfall.

The committee gave me the go-ahead. Donald Trump's people were somewhat dubious. (I suppose they don't get many requests from youth pastors for exclusive use of the architectural showpiece of their $500 million building. Yet they eventually said yes and I thought we were all set: incredible desserts at tables set around the Marble Terrace Cafe at the base of the waterfall while soft music plays, 10:30 p.m., Friday night, June 3.

The banquet went reasonably well, the chartered bus was on time, the normal weekend late-night traffic tie up at the Lincoln Tunnel was no worse than expected, and we arrived right at 10:30 p.m. in all our dressed-up finery. It's an awesome sight: New York City, midtown Manhattan, Fifth Avenue, Trump Tower between Saks Fifth Avenue and FAO Schwartz. The huge flags of Trump's Plaza Hotel across the street were gently swaying in the breeze as we got off our bus. Fifth Avenue was a river of limousines and taxi cabs.

As we entered Trump Tower, I counted seven security guards in tuxedoes, nervously fingering their walkie-talkies. We made our way down to the Marble Terrace Cafe. I quickly inquired of our host why the waterfall was dry.

"Oh, I'm sorry Mr. Kageler, that's turned off until the morning."

"Well, please turn it back on. This is why we came. I told them all about this and we're expecting it to be on."

"Oh, I'm sorry Mr. Kageler, that won't be possible."

To make a long story short, the waterfall stayed dry. The Trump people on site did try to compensate by making it an all-you-can eat dessert instead of single servings.

It was hard for me to switch from being mad at the snafu to being grateful that, all in all, the night was going well. The kids were having a good time and I had only heard one youth group member swear at another, so the evening represented significant progress in the few months I'd been there! Eventually, I was able to re-enter the relational flow of the evening and join in the celebration.

Enjoying what we have as youth workers is critical to growing a healthy youth ministry. It only takes a few seconds for kids to perceive if we're upset, dissatisfied, bored, or distracted. We don't have a hope of growing a healthy group if we can't have an attitude of gratitude as we engage in this wonderful thing called youth ministry.

Let's look at how we can enjoy what we have and enjoy the journey as we seek to grow our youth group.

KEEP THE BIG PICTURE IN FOCUS

Whether we have four, forty, or four hundred youth in our ministries, we must remember these are individual young people, not statistics. It is an awesome privilege to have the opportunity to do kingdom work. Giving spiritual direction is one of the highest callings there is.

So many times I've heard youth workers exclaim in amazement over the joyful privilege of youth ministry—to lead kids—go skiing with them, counsel them, eat pepperoni pizza with them, see them "get it," and pass it on.

It doesn't always turn out how we hope. But I pray our hearts will see from a higher-ground perspective, looking beyond dry indoor waterfalls, hay-embedded carpets, and missing VCRs.

A great benefit of youth work is that it forces us to deal with our own spirituality, or lack thereof. Youth ministry is too hard to do in our own strength. As we are confronted with our own fruit-of-the-Spirit shortcomings, we either get on our knees or get out. I can thankfully tell you that 1979 was last time I was so angry with youth group members (over a prank turned life threatening) that I swore. There have been many situations just as terrible since, but I've deepened in the Lord enough not to lash out with verbal abuse.

ENJOY YOUR PEERS

Enjoy those alongside you in the ministry. Read Psalm 139 and thank him for his creativity in designing each of us.

Take every opportunity you can to attend youth worker seminars and conventions. It's a visual and tangible reminder that God uses all types, shapes, and sizes in growing youth ministries. Only a tiny percent of the people we'll see in these settings is the seeming ideal: former pro-football player, guitar virtuoso, perfect blend of Lion-Otter-Golden Retriever-Beaver, with a by-the-side spouse and two perfect children. The rest we'll see are very imperfect, just like us. Yet God uses us all, week by week, all around the country. We're part of a Great Commission movement and God is using us to make a difference!

BE THANKFUL FOR WHO DOES SHOW UP

Remember Tami in Chapter Two, who was drop-jaw astounded that only twelve of my one hundred fifty senior highers attended the big event? I learned early in youth ministry that the larger the group, the smaller the percentage that shows up at any given time. I learned the other side of the coin too: my days were numbered in youth work if I felt bad about who didn't come instead of glad about those who did. Of course we want kids to show up, and we'd like those not present to be present, but if we get mentally hung up on the nonattenders, we won't be able to give full attention to the youth in front of our noses.

Kids have a natural ability to sense what we really feel. The Otter in me longs to see every single kid at every single thing we do in youth ministry so they can tangibly feel my delight in their presence. I'm not communicating they are doing me a favor by coming or that they should come out of duty to me or the program. I do, though, want them to know that they matter to me and other leaders.

This requires tremendous internal flexibility and a servant heart. These don't come naturally. They only come with increased Christlikeness and dependence on God.

In a growing youth ministry, there will be newcomers who stick and newcomers who slide off. Yes, we are sorry they don't all become solid members of the group, but we should be tremendously glad for those who are integrated into the ministry we lead.

REMEMBER WHEN WE WERE KIDS

It's helpful to remember our own past. Were we in any way obnoxious as teenagers? If so, did caring adults help us get through our rough years? If this is the case, we can especially enjoy the fact now that we get to help others as we ourselves have been helped.

CELEBRATE THE JOURNEY

There is a sign on my bulletin board which states:

> **Gifts to Give Those Around Me:**
>
> **Joy**
> **Kindness**
> **Enthusiasm**
> **Gratitude**
> **Wonder**

It is especially the wonder that causes me to enjoy this adolescent conglomerate I stand in front of week by week. It is a wonder to see little increments of personal growth as the months go by. These serve as down payments, surety that maturity is indeed on its way.

Recently I attended the awards assembly for Nyack Middle School. Many of our youth ministry members marched across the stage receiving awards for honor roll, high honor holl, principal's award, and the like. Four years from now they will march across a stage down the street to receive their high school diplomas, and four years later they will very likely receive college degrees. I admit that is a long time away, but at least I know the process of growing up is taking place.

Enjoying the journey means being thankful God has given us the chance to be involved in at least a small slice of kids' lives.

TREASURE THE MOUNTAIN TOPS

I was laying on my back in the Cascade Mountains. It was a warm summer night and the mosquitoes had gone to bed hours ago. On this cabinet backpack trip, we were far from the van and civilization. As midnight came and went we counted satellites and shooting stars, and prayed, and sang. We thanked God for the privilege of side-by-side ministry. We poured our hearts out to God about the coming school year. Our eyes were riveted on the majesty of the Milky Way-filled night sky, and our hearts were connected as we lay side by side. It was one of those mountain top experiences!

In youth ministry, we don't get these mountain-top experiences every week. But they do happen as we hang in there, enjoying the troops he has given us and working to see our youth ministry become healthy and growing. Creating this kind of youth ministry does not come easy; there are many roadblocks. Yet as we see the roadblocks cleared away, we can exclaim as Paul did so enthusiastically, "Now unto him who is able to do immeasurably more than all we ask or imagine . . . to him be glory in the church and in Christ Jesus throughout all generations, for ever and ever! Amen" (Ephesians 3:20-21).

WHY GROUPS ARE GROWING

- "Prayer and the kids' excitement about God!" *(Minnesota)*
- "It's a combination of the Holy Spirit, hungry kids, strong leadership, positive events." *(Wisconsin)*
- "We started a group for third through sixth graders. We had no regular junior and senior highers. This group averages twelve to fifteen a week, never wanting to miss! Now we have a junior high group of five which will keep growing. It is exciting for our church! We started a youth choir too!" *(Mississippi)*

WHY GROUPS ARE NOT GROWING

- "Discontinuation of high school programming and leadership burnout (that was me)." *(California)*

FOR WHAT IT'S WORTH

- "We're providing more structure in Sunday school, including regular Bible study, journaling, team teaching, getting to know kids more personally, and providing both Girls' Night Out and Boys' Night Out events in addition to combined events. Kids are now bringing friends to Sunday school as well as special events." *(California)*

NOTES

NOTES

NOTES

NOTES